GW00771499

ULTIMATE BEGINNER SERIES®
BLUEGRASS
BANJO *Basics*

by Dennis Caplinger

Alfred Publishing Co., Inc.
16320 Roscoe Blvd., Suite 100
P.O. Box 10003
Van Nuys, CA 91410-0003
alfred.com

ISBN-10: 0-7692-8544-9 (Book & CD)
ISBN-13: 978-0-7692-8544-3 (Book & CD)

CONTENTS

INTRODUCTION

This book is designed to help you learn to play the five-string banjo in the three-finger bluegrass style. If you are a beginner, that's great—we'll start from scratch and cover all the bases. If you already play a little, that's okay, too—there are some good versions of tunes here, as well as some basic tips on how to play with other people in a band context.

ABOUT THE CD

All of the music examples and tunes are included on the CD. It is very important for you to listen to the music as much as possible in order to really get a feel for the way these tunes are supposed to sound. There really is no way to notate adequately on paper all the subtle nuances of this music, so *listen, listen, listen!*

The tunes on the CD are mixed so that the band is on the left side of the stereo field and the banjo is on the right by itself. By panning the music hard left, the banjo disappears so that you can be the only banjo playing along. Panning the music hard right will solo up the banjo so that you can study it in detail without hearing the other instruments. The CD track number is listed at the top of each example for easy reference.

PARTS OF THE BANJO

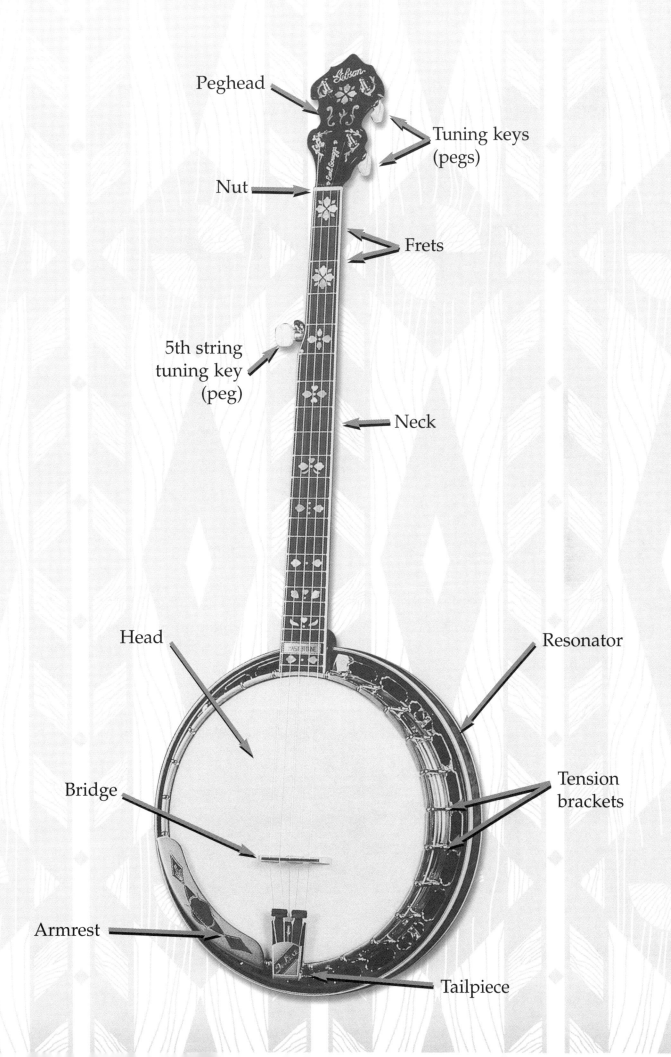

Peghead

Tuning keys (pegs)

Nut

Frets

5th string tuning key (peg)

Neck

Head

Resonator

Bridge

Tension brackets

Armrest

Tailpiece

TUNING THE BANJO

CD
2

Tuning to a Keyboard

The five strings of a banjo can be tuned to a keyboard by matching the sound of each open banjo string to the keyboard notes, as indicated in the diagram.

Note: You will hear the intonation better, and your banjo will stay in better tune, if you loosen the strings and tune them **up** to pitch rather than bringing them from the pitch and tuning down.

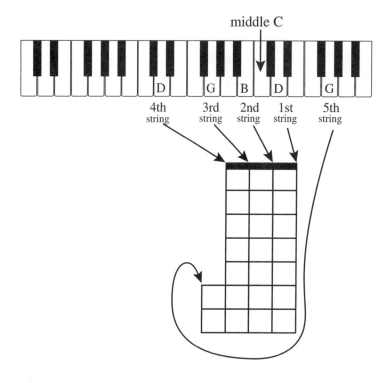

Electronic Tuners

Many brands of small battery-operated tuners are available. These are excellent for keeping your banjo in perfect tune and for developing your ear to hear intonation very accurately. Simply follow the instructions supplied with the tuner.

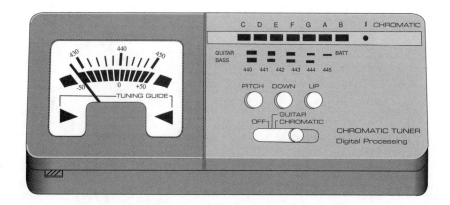

TUNING THE BANJO TO ITSELF

- Tune your 4th string (D) to a piano or some other instrument.
- Depress the 4th string at the 5th fret. Play it and you will hear the note G, which is the same as the 3rd string played open. Turn the 3rd string tuning key until the pitch of the open 3rd string (G) matches that of the 4th string/5th fret (also G).
- Depress the 3rd string at the 4th fret. Play it and you will hear the note B, which is the same as the 2nd string played open. Turn the 2nd string tuning key until the pitch of the open 2nd string (B) matches that of the 3rd string/4th fret (also B).
- Depress the 2nd string at the 3rd fret. Play it and you will hear the note D, which is the same as the 1st string played open. Turn the 1st string tuning key until the pitch of the open 1st string (D) matches that of the 2nd string/3rd fret (also D).
- Depress the 1st string at the 5th fret. Play it and you will hear the note G, which is the same as the 5th string played open. Turn the 5th string tuning key until the pitch of the open 5th string (G) matches that of the 1st string/5th fret (also G).

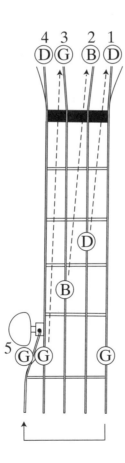

READING THE MUSIC EXAMPLES IN THIS BOOK

Example 1

Here is a sample measure that includes eighth and quarter notes:

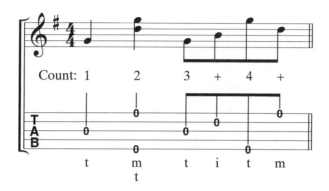

The count shown in this example won't appear in every tune, but we will include it in the first few examples in order to give you an idea of how to count time. Each count (number) is equal to one beat (quarter note), and the alternate eighth notes fall on "and." The letters (t, i, m, etc.) refer to the right hand:

t = thumb
i = index
m = middle

You will notice that we have included standard notation along with all the tablature in this book. This is a significant departure from most other banjo instructional books. Our rationale for this is that music notation may make the learning process easier for students who are familiar with it or for students who are learning banjo after already studying another instrument (like guitar or violin, for example). For those folks who don't care to learn about or use music notation, that's okay, too. The tablature system is a great way to learn and is actually the most common way to learn to play five-string bluegrass-style banjo. Using either method along with the enclosed CD will yield good results.

For more in-depth information on music notation and tab, see the appendix at the end of the book.

UNIT 1: SOME BASICS

There are a few things you'll need to have in order to work your way through this book. First, you need to be playing a five-string banjo. The playing techniques for four-string banjo are totally different, so make sure you have that 5th-string peg sticking out halfway up the neck. Make sure that the banjo you're playing is in good condition. I always advise students to have a reputable luthier look at their instruments before they get started. Playing the banjo is difficult enough without having to fight with an instrument that is poorly set up. There are many adjustable parts to a banjo, and like an automobile engine, if the parts are not adjusted correctly, it won't work properly. Even the most famous players often have their instruments professionally set up, so don't be afraid to have someone look at your banjo if it needs it.

You'll be learning to pick the strings using the thumb, index finger, and middle finger of your right hand (t, i, and m). It's okay to start out picking with just your bare fingers, but you should get used to using picks as soon as possible. You'll need to get a plastic thumbpick and two metal fingerpicks. There are several different brands to choose from, so check out your local music store and see what's available. Picks come in various sizes and materials. Make sure your thumbpick is plastic and the finger-picks are metal. This will help you get the best tone and volume out of your banjo. Your thumbpick should fit snugly enough so that it doesn't turn on your thumb when you pick the string. You can fit the two metal fingerpicks to your index and middle fingers by bending the sides around until they are snug. You can also bend the flat surface of the fingerpicks up around the tips of your fingers to adjust the angle at which the picks strike the strings. For now, just try to make your picks look like mine in these photos:

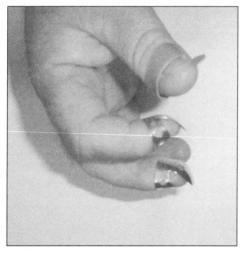 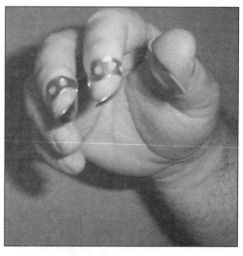

Get a strap for your banjo. Even though you'll probably be learning to pick while sitting, a strap will help you balance the weight of the banjo and keep you from having to support the neck with your left hand. I like to use a leather strap and attach it to the tension hooks like this:

 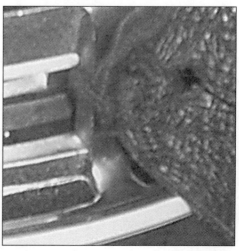

Wear the strap over your left shoulder and adjust the length of the strap so that the banjo sits comfortably and solidly in your lap without slipping. Angle the neck up slightly like this:

One of the most important things to remember about learning to play the banjo is that everyone's body is different. What may be comfortable for someone else may not be right for you. Try to position the banjo and your hands so that they approximate the position in the photos you see here.

Right-Hand Position
Place your right hand on the banjo like this:

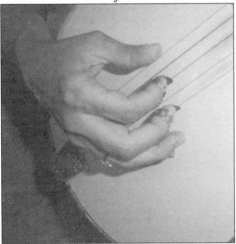 

It is very important that you keep your ring and little fingers anchored to the banjo head just in front of the bridge. This can be awkward at first, but it will help keep your picking hand stable. Try to keep your hand and wrist relaxed: this will help keep your picking smooth and even.

Left-Hand Position
Place your left hand on the neck of the banjo like this:

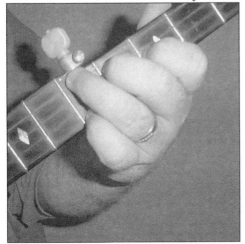 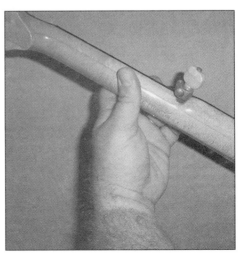

It is important to try to keep the thumb of your left hand on the back of the banjo neck as shown in the photo. Resist the temptation to lay the neck in the palm of your hand. Proper left-hand placement will allow you to develop good fingering technique and help build speed.

UNIT 2: BANJO ROLLS

THE RIGHT HAND

We'll get started by learning some basic right-hand patterns, or rolls. Learning to play these rolls cleanly and smoothly is the most important part of learning to pick the banjo. I will describe these basics in detail to help you learn the basic movements of your right-hand fingers. The best way to practice these rolls is to start very slowly and evenly, playing each pattern over and over many times. Concentrate on counting each beat and try not to speed up or slow down. Remember: speed only comes with practice!

Example 2: The Pinch

- Thumb picks down on 5th string
- Index picks up on 2nd string
- Middle picks up on 1st string

Pick all three strings at the same time, making sure to keep your ring and little fingers down on the head in front of the bridge.

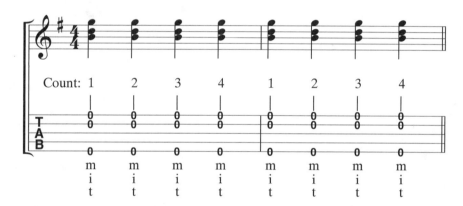

Example 3: Basic Pinch Rhythm

- Beat 1: Thumb picks down on 3rd string
- Beat 2: Pinch: Thumb picks down on 5th string
  Index picks up on 2nd string
  Middle picks up on 1st string
- Beat 3: Thumb picks down on 4th string
- Beat 4: Pinch

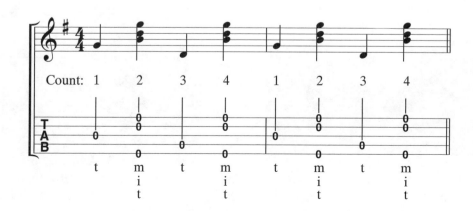

ROLL PATTERNS

In the following four examples you will learn four basic roll patterns. These four roll patterns are the backbone of most bluegrass banjo picking. Eventually you should be able to mix and match these patterns—flowing from one to another to suit the demands of the melody and the feel of the song. Study each of these patterns carefully. Memorize them!

Example 4: Forward Roll

- Thumb picks down on 5th string
- Index picks up on 2nd string
- Middle picks up on 1st string

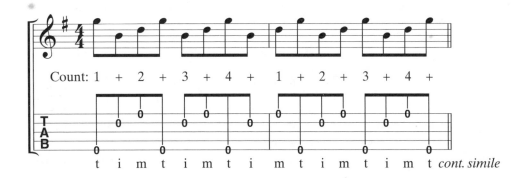

Example 5: Backward Roll

- Middle picks up on 1st string
- Index picks up on 2nd string
- Thumb picks down on 5th string

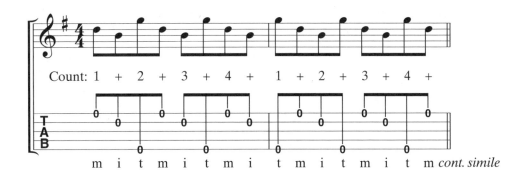

Example 6: Forward-Backward Roll

- Thumb picks down on 3rd string
- Index picks up on 2nd string
- Middle picks up on 1st string
- Thumb picks down on 5th string
- Middle picks up on 1st string
- Index picks up on 2nd string
- Thumb picks down on 3rd string
- Middle picks up on 1st string

You will notice that this roll is an eight-note pattern. Be sure to play all eight notes before repeating the pattern.

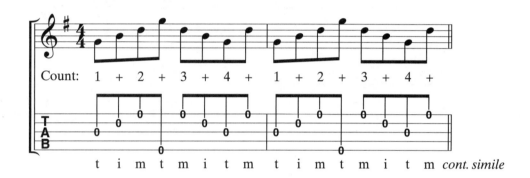

Example 7: Alternating Thumb Roll

- Thumb picks down on 3rd string
- Index picks up on 2nd string
- Thumb picks down on 5th string
- Middle picks up on 1st string

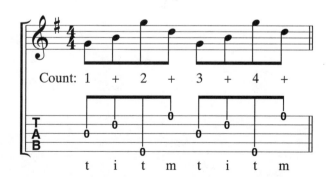

The previous roll patterns are the basics of bluegrass banjo playing. We will explore other rolls later in the book, but for now, practice these patterns over and over until you begin to feel comfortable with them.

14

LEFT-HAND BASICS

Now that you have some right-hand basics, let's look at a few left-hand chords. Remember to try to keep your left-hand thumb in the middle of the back of the banjo neck. Put your left-hand fingers down right behind the appropriate fret as shown in the chord diagrams:

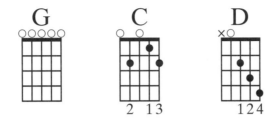

To practice making these chords, place your fingers on the appropriate fret and string as per the diagrams, and then pick each note of the chord individually with your right-hand thumb. Make sure that each individual note rings clear and clean. If the note is muted or buzzing, rearrange your finger position until the note is clear. When all the notes of the chord sound clean, then lightly strum all the strings together with your right-hand thumb. Now practice changing from one chord to another: G to C to D and back to G, over and over until you can change from one to another easily and cleanly. Try not to hit the 5th string with your right-hand thumb when playing the D chord; the open 5th string is a G note, which is not part of a D chord. Just leave the 5th string out of the D chord for now.

PUTTING BOTH HANDS TOGETHER

Now that you have a handle on some right- and left-hand basics, let's try putting the hands together so we can begin to make some real music. Remember to take things very slowly at first—it will take awhile to develop coordination between your hands. If you encounter difficulty, go back to practicing the left- and right-hand skills separately; then try putting them together when you feel comfortable. Even the best players sometimes work on the hands separately if they are trying to solve problem areas in their playing.

Example 8

In this example, we will combine the right-hand pinch with the basic G, C, and D chords. We will change to a new chord every two measures with the left hand. The right-hand pattern is the same for the G and C chords, but when we make the D chord, we will avoid playing the 5th string. Instead, drop your thumb down and hit the 3rd string.

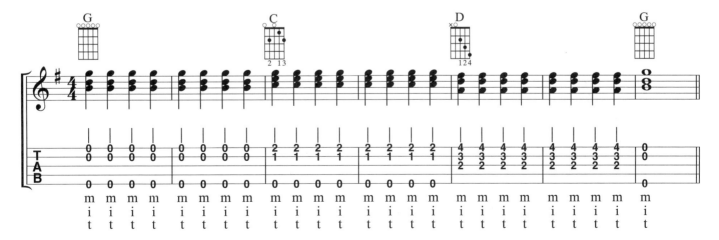

Example 9

Now we'll keep the same left-hand chord changes, but we'll combine them with the basic pinch rhythm in the right hand.

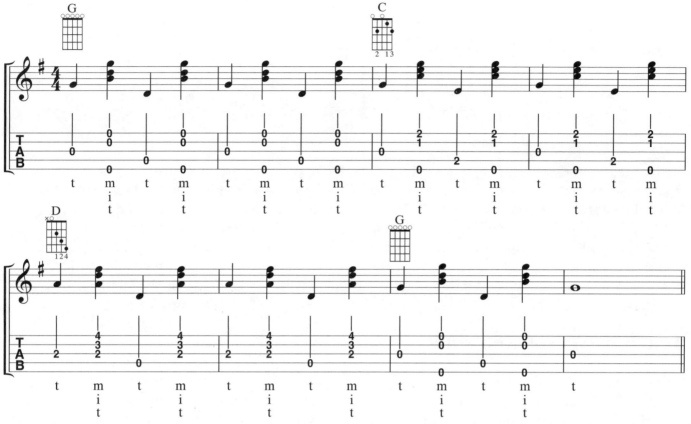

Example 10

Next, let's use the alternating thumb pattern in the right hand.

16

All right, this is really starting to sound like banjo picking now. Notice the two quarter-note rests in the last measure of Example 10, on beats 2 and 4; you'll be seeing a lot of these. Don't forget to count: timing is extremely important. Also, you may have noticed that I have you hitting the open 5th string while you're rolling through a D chord in measures 5 and 6. In this case, the sound of the open 5th string ringing across the other notes of the chord is kind of pretty. It works because the notes of the chord are not being played simultaneously, as in the previous examples. When the notes of a chord are played individually like this, the musical term for it is an *arpeggio*. We play a lot of arpeggios on the banjo because of the nature of our right-hand picking techniques.

CD

10

Example 11

Let's do one more using this same chord progression. This time we'll use the forward-backward roll.

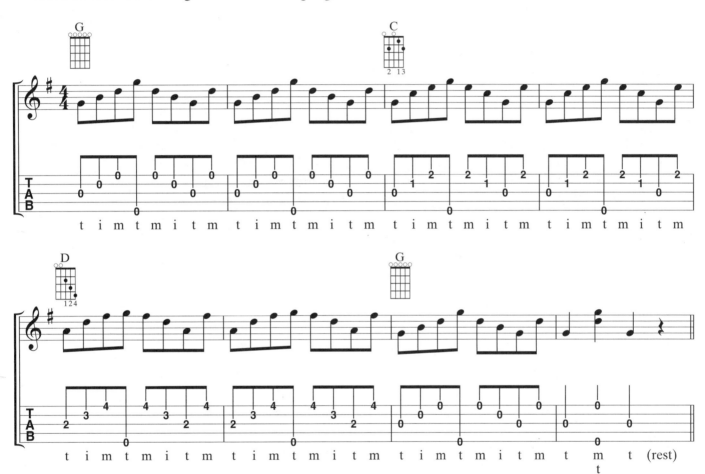

Don't forget that you cannot practice the above examples, exercises, rolls, and chords too much. Practice, practice, practice! Strive to play evenly and don't forget to count. Sooner or later, you'll develop a sense of timing so that you feel the beat and don't have to count out loud. One excellent exercise is to play a single roll (like the forward roll, for example) over and over for a minute without stopping, concentrating on not missing any of the strings and playing as evenly as possible. If you think a minute isn't a long time, just try it!

Example 12: "Boil the Cabbage Down"

Now it's time to play our first real song, "Boil the Cabbage Down." This song is an old-time fiddle tune that we'll play with the band later. The right-hand pattern is basically a forward roll, but the roll starts with the index finger instead of the thumb. Pay attention to the way the roll changes at the end of each measure. The repeat sign at the end of the song indicates to repeat the song back from the beginning. After the second time through, just end; don't repeat again. Once again, take it slow and count.

BOIL THE CABBAGE DOWN

TRADITIONAL

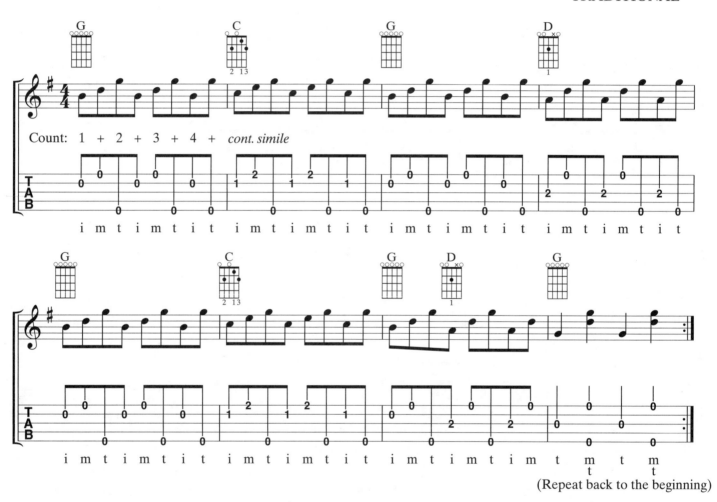

(Repeat back to the beginning)

UNIT 3: SCRUGGS-STYLE BANJO

The rolls and exercises that you've been working on are preparing you to play in a three-finger bluegrass style, which is commonly called **Scruggs-style** banjo picking. Although he didn't invent three-fingered picking, Earl Scruggs is credited with refining and popularizing this style of picking while working as a member of Bill Monroe's Bluegrass Boys in the 1940s and later with Flatt and Scruggs and the Foggy Mountain Boys through the late 1960s. Earl is still performing today and considered to be one of the elder statesmen of bluegrass music. I highly recommend that you try to find and listen to as much banjo music as possible, especially anything that features the playing of Earl Scruggs. There are many wonderful players out there these days, but Earl's playing truly defines the genre of bluegrass banjo.

One of the most interesting aspects of Scruggs-style picking is the way in which the melody is integrated into the right-hand rolls. If you watch a really good banjo player, you'll notice that it seems like his right hand is doing a lot more work than his left hand most of the time. Here's the concept: Find the melody with your left hand on the neck and then adapt your right-hand rolls to render that melody. You could say that the right hand is a "slave to the left." The left hand finds the pitches of the melody and the right hand does whatever it takes to make those notes come out with the proper rhythm and articulation. There are always various ways to play a given melody, and individual players will hear things differently and use different rolls to produce their versions of a tune. That's one reason why people develop different styles. The more you listen to good players, the more you'll begin to hear the sometimes subtle differences in their styles.

Example 13: "Oh Susanna" (Basic melody)

Let's look at an example of a simple melody, the first few bars of "Oh Susanna."

OH SUSANNA

TRADITIONAL

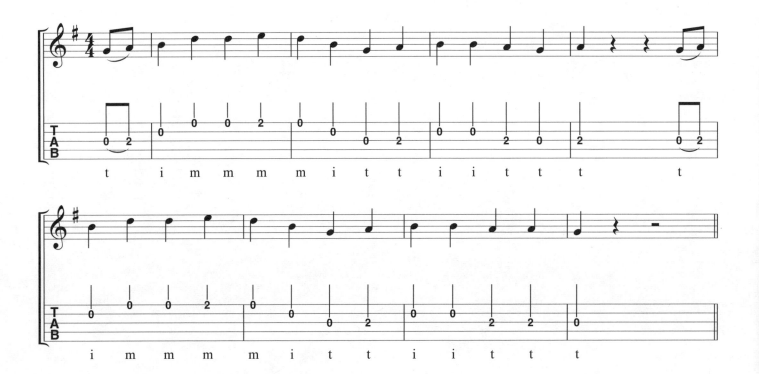

20

12B **Example 14: "Oh Susanna" (Scruggs version)**

Here's the same tune, but played in a Scruggs-style version.

OH SUSANNA

TRADITIONAL

Notice how you can still hear the melody even though it's now within a roll. That's the basic idea.
Note: We'll study the "slides" and "hammers" used in this arrangement in the following examples.

LEFT-HAND TECHNIQUES: The Slide

Some of the neatest sounds you can make on the banjo come from the combination of right-hand rolls with various left-hand embellishments or ornaments. A lot of the characteristic sound of bluegrass banjo comes from these left-hand techniques, which you can use to make a basic melody more interesting.

13A **Example 15**

Try this: Put the middle finger of your left hand on the 2nd fret of the 3rd string. Pick the string with your right-hand thumb, and then immediately slide your left hand up the neck so that your middle finger moves from the 2nd to the 4th fret. Keep your middle finger down on the string so you can hear the note "slide" from one pitch to the next. You pick only the first note—the second note is the result of the slide. Notice in the tab that a slide is notated with a slur mark (pick only the first note) and a diagonal slide indication showing the slide from one note to the next.

21

Example 16

This time we slide from the 2nd to the 5th fret on the 4th string. You can slide on any string, using any finger.

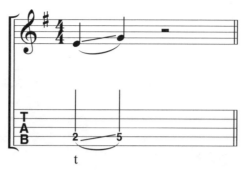

Now let's combine some slides with some right-hand exercises.

Example 17

Here are some slides and pinches together. Use the middle finger of your left hand for the slide. Remember to take it slowly and count accurately. Keep good pressure on the finger that's doing the slide. Try to make the slurred note (second note) as loud as the picked note (first note).

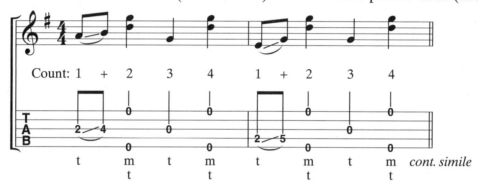

Example 18

Now we'll incorporate the slides into some right-hand rolls. Here is a slide on the 3rd string done inside an alternating thumb roll.

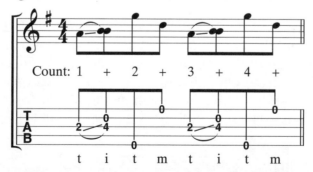

In this example, you pick the open 2nd string with your right hand at exactly the same time that you arrive at the top of the slide (4th fret) with your left. Try to make this slide happen within the framework of the right-hand roll; don't mess up your right-hand timing waiting on the slide. If you have problems, try taking the slide out of the roll. Play the roll without the slide and get the timing of the roll working properly—count! Then put the slide into the roll with the correct timing.

Example 19

Here's a forward-backward roll with a slide in it.

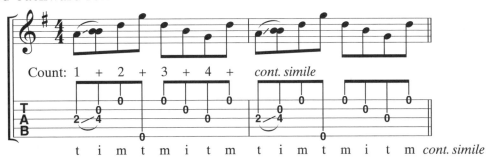

Example 20

This is a common roll pattern with a slide and a pinch.

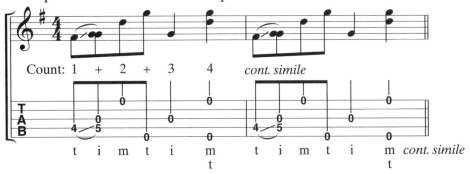

Example 21

Here's another version of "Boil the Cabbage Down" using some slides.

BOIL THE CABBAGE DOWN

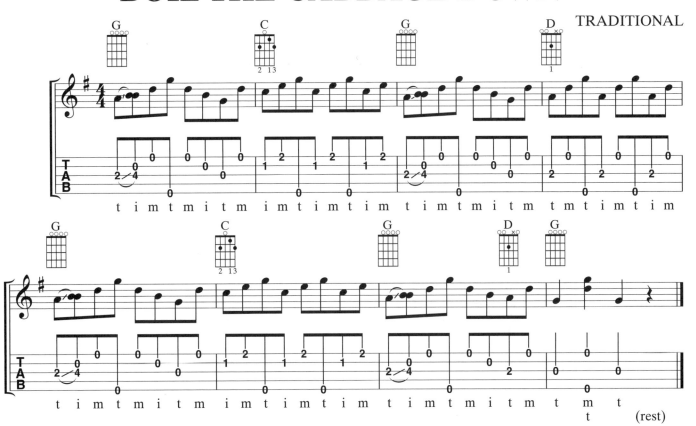

LEFT-HAND TECHNIQUES: The Hammer-On

Example 22

The next left-hand technique we'll look at is the hammer, or hammer-on. Get your left hand ready for this technique. Hold the middle finger of your left hand over the top of the 2nd fret of the 4th string, but don't touch it yet. Pick the 4th string with your right-hand thumb; then immediately hammer your middle finger down onto the 4th string at the 2nd fret. You pick only the first note; the hammering down of your middle finger onto the string sounds the second note. The hammer is used whenever you have an upward slur that is not a slide (play the first note and hammer your finger down on the next note).

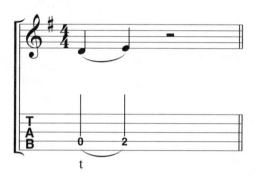

Example 23

As with the slide, the object when hammering a note is to get the second note (which is not picked with the right hand) to be as loud as the first note (which is picked by the right hand).

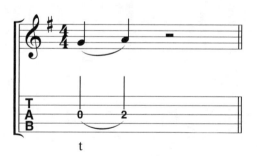

Example 24

It is possible to pick a note simultaneously with the hammer. Here are some examples.

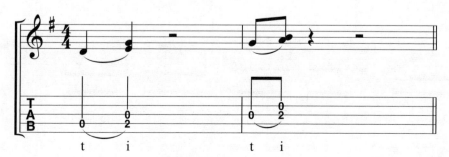

24

Example 25

Try to make the hammer happen at exactly the same moment you pick the second note. Another very common technique is to fret a note with a left-hand finger and then while still holding that note, hammer with a different left-hand finger.

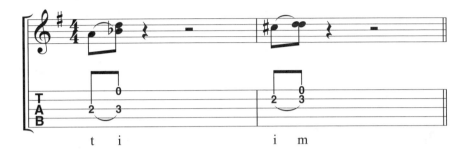

In both of the previous examples, the note on the 2nd fret was held down by the left-hand index finger, and the hammer was performed by the left-hand middle finger. When you do a hammer like this, the left-hand index finger should remain down on the string even after the middle finger hammers.

Example 26

Here are some hammer exercises using rolls.

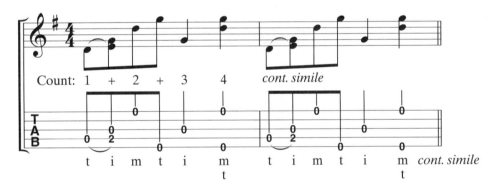

Example 27

You may have heard this lick before; it is the opening of "Foggy Mountain Breakdown," a very famous bluegrass tune popularized by Earl Scruggs.

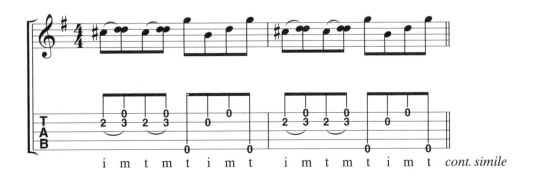

Now it's time for another tune. This one features both slides and hammers. It's called
"Cumberland Gap." There is a D chord implied in measure 4 even though we don't finger a D chord.

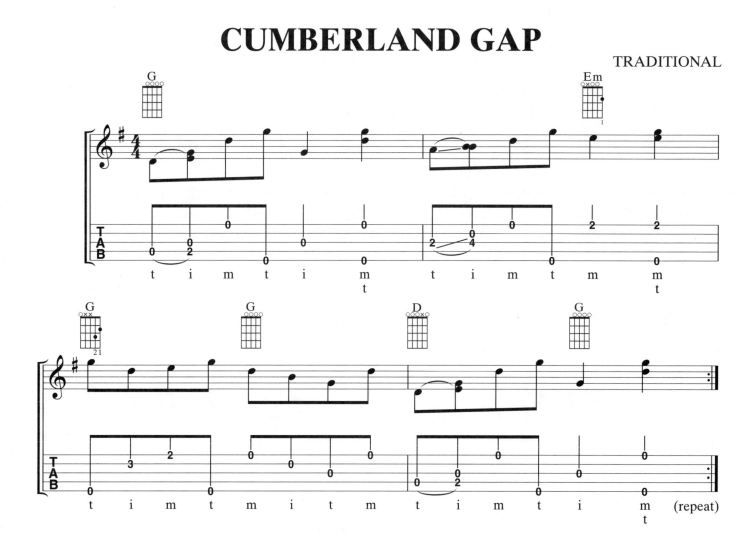

CUMBERLAND GAP

TRADITIONAL

LEFT-HAND TECHNIQUES: The Pull-Off

Example 29

The pull-off is another technique you will use a lot. Basically, this technique is the exact opposite of the hammer-on technique. Put your left-hand middle finger on the 2nd fret of the 4th string. Pick the 4th string with your right-hand thumb and then immediately snap your left-hand middle finger off of the string in the direction of your palm. When done correctly, the second note will be almost as loud and clear as the first note.

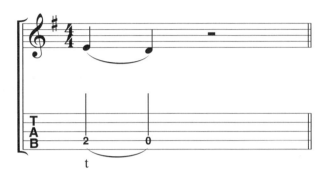

Example 30

Here are some more pull-offs.

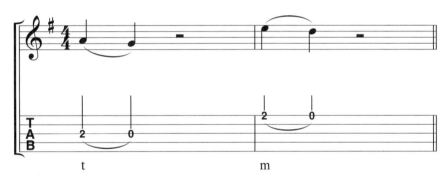

Example 31

As with the other techniques, it is possible to pick another string at the same time as you execute the pull-off.

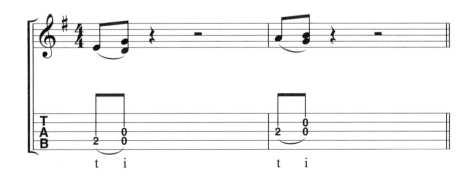

Example 32

You can also pull off from one finger to another:

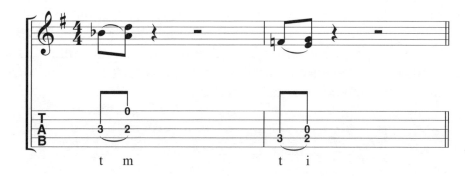

In both of the above examples, the left-hand index should be on the 2nd fret and the middle finger should be on the 3rd fret of the string at the same time; then pull the middle finger off while leaving the index finger firmly planted on the 2nd fret. Strive to make the pull-off happen at exactly the same time you pick the second note with your right hand.

Example 33

Examples 33 and 34 are pull-offs combined with some rolls.

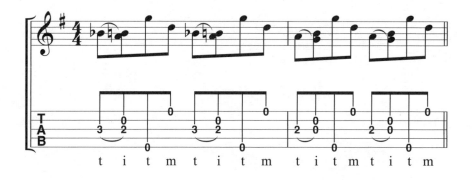

Example 34

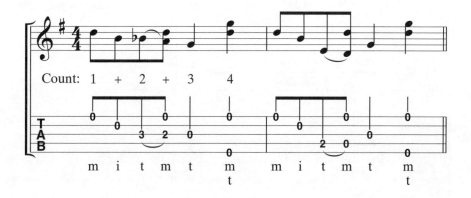

Example 35: "Cripple Creek"

Now that you have a firm grasp of all three left-hand techniques—the slide, hammer-on, and pull-off—let's try a tune that combines all of them. Here's "Cripple Creek"—this arrangement uses a variety of rolls and embellishments and has a real bluegrass sound.

CRIPPLE CREEK

TRADITIONAL

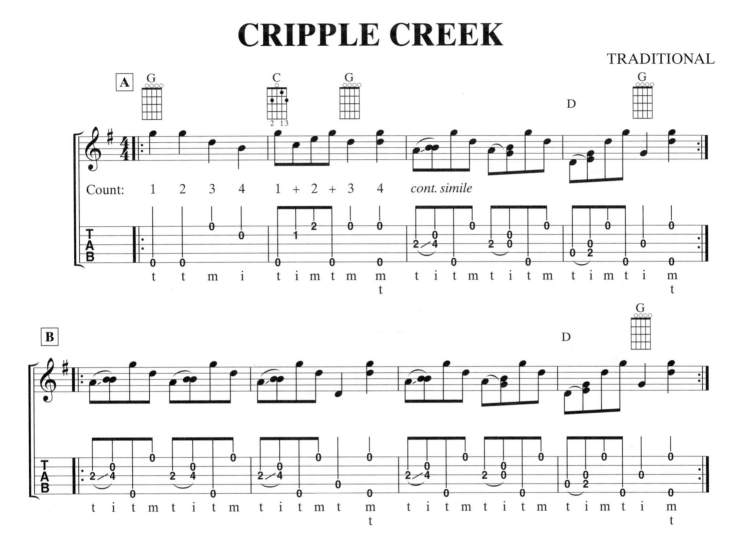

Congratulations! If you can play "Cripple Creek," you are well on your way to becoming a bluegrass banjo player.

UNIT 4: MOVING ON

Let's move on to a few tunes that use all the techniques you've learned up to now, with some new twists and turns thrown in to make things interesting. You will notice that from now on, the right-hand roll patterns used will be less repetitive and the use of left-hand ornaments will become more prominent. This is all part of the "right hand being a slave to the left" idea described earlier. The next song is called "Old Joe Clark," and it includes an F chord (measure 13):

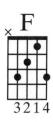

Example 36

Practice this chord like you did the others before you attempt to play the tune. There is also a right-hand roll you haven't seen yet (measures 1, 3, and 5).

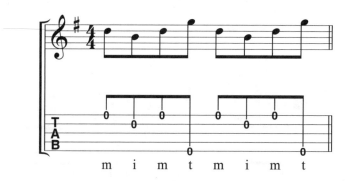

Example 37: "Old Joe Clark"

Notice that the first two notes of the tablature happen before the first full measure of the tune. These notes are called "pickup" notes. To start the tune, count "1 2 3" and then play the two pickup notes as "4 and." Also, like many other bluegrass tunes (especially fiddle tunes), this one has a musical form called AABB. In other words, you play the first section (labeled A) twice, followed by the second section (labeled B) twice. In order to facilitate writing this form down on paper, we use a system of first and second endings. To play this tune through completely, follow this form:
- Start at the beginning.
- Play Section A to the end of measure 8 (first ending repeat sign).
- Go back to letter A (repeat sign at beginning of measure 1; don't repeat the pickup notes at the very beginning of the tune).
- Play Section A again to the end of measure 7, skip the first ending, and go directly to the second ending. Now you have played Section A twice.
- Next, play Section B from letter B to the end of the tune (repeat sign), and then repeat back to letter B (repeat sign) and play it a gain until the end. Now you have played Section B twice: AABB.

OLD JOE CLARK

TRADITIONAL

"Salt Creek" is another popular tune in AABB form—just follow the repeat signs. Once again you will use the F chord (measures 3 and 4) and a new version of the F chord that occurs higher up the neck (measures 11 and 12):

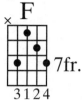

Study this chord position carefully. At first glance, it may appear to be the same as the first F chord you learned, but it is different. The placement of the left-hand index and middle fingers has changed. Have fun with "Salt Creek"!

SALT CREEK

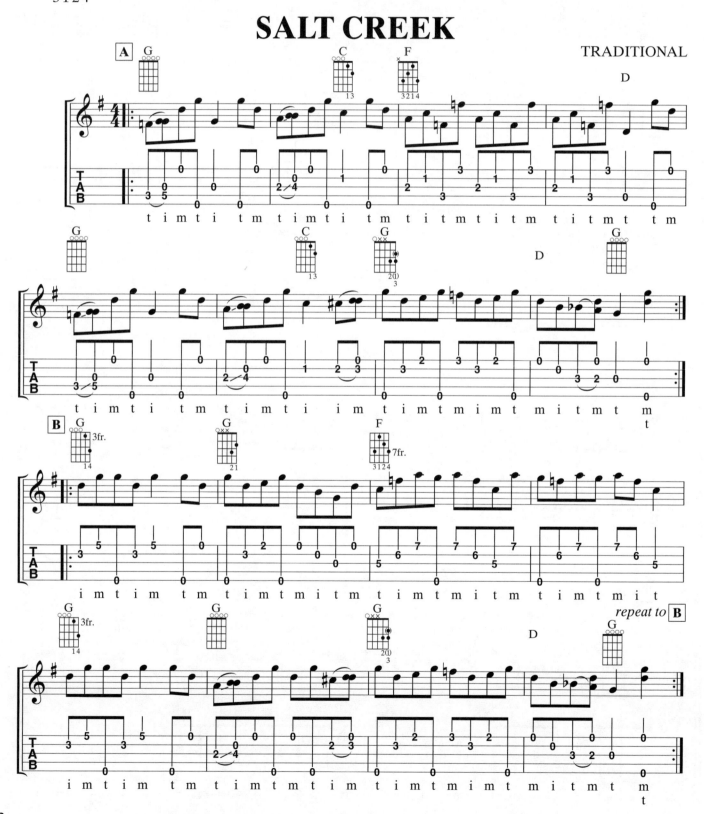

32

Quite a number of the songs that have become instrumental bluegrass standards come from old-time Appalachian mountain music. In fact, just about every tune in this book falls into that category and many of them have lyrics. "John Hardy" tells the story of an outlaw on the run:

> *John Hardy was a desperate little man*
> *He wore his guns every day*
> *He shot down a man on the West Virginia line*
> *You should've seen John Hardy getting away, oh Lord,*
> *You should've seen John Hardy getting away.*

This tune is not in an AABB format, so just play it from the top, and when you get to the end repeat back to letter A and play it over and over. There are three pickup notes out front—beat 1 is a rest and you start playing the first pickup note on beat 2. There is a very famous Scruggs-style lick that happens in the next-to-last measure (19):

Example 39: Scruggs-Style Lick

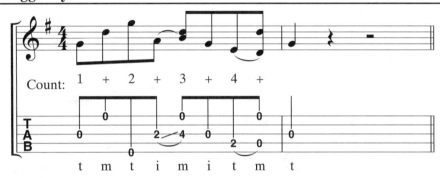

Once again, if you have trouble with this lick, take the left hand completely out and practice the right-hand roll by itself. Make sure to count correctly. Variations of this lick occur in measures 3 and 11. There is also a new chord called a D7 (measures 13, 15, and 17), and it looks like this:

Example 40: "John Hardy"

Be sure to pay attention to the left-hand fingering diagrams. Using the correct left-hand fingers to get the notes will make things a lot easier.

JOHN HARDY

TRADITIONAL

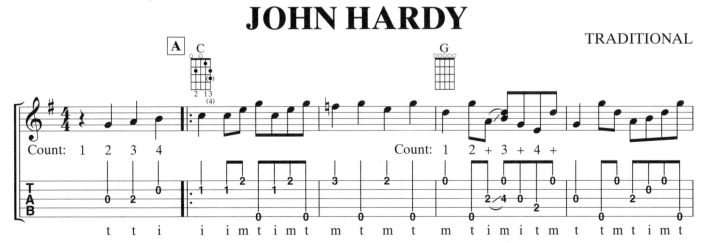

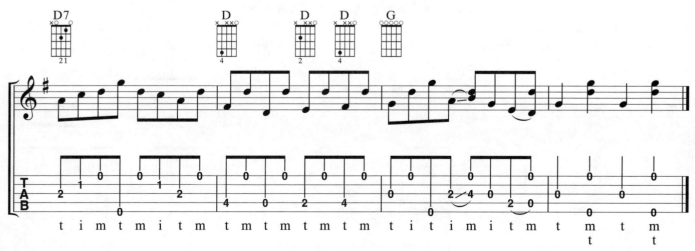

34

UNIT 5: PLAYING BACKUP

One of the most enjoyable things about making music is being able to play with other people. The interaction among the various instruments in a bluegrass band is a big part of what defines the music—that is, what makes it sound bluegrass. Each instrument has a unique role in the band sound, depending on whether it is playing lead or backup. In a typical bluegrass setting, only one of the instruments in the group will be playing a solo at any given time. This is not always true of other forms of music. In Irish music, for example, it is very common for everyone to be playing the melody together at the same time. Learning to play backup is very important when you're in a group setting because if you are jamming with other pickers and singers, most of your time will be spent supporting other players. You can (and should) spend as much time as you'd like studying the art of playing backup. There are many different types of backup, but the single most important skill to learn is how to play good, solid rhythm.

Basic Backup Rhythm: Vamping
We will be using closed chords to play rhythm. A closed chord is one in which there are no open strings. All the strings (except the 5th string) will be fretted. Because all the strings are fretted, we can move the chord anywhere up or down the neck. For the most part we will not be using the 5th string when playing rhythm backup.

Because there are many ways to make any given chord on the banjo, it is helpful to focus on the shape of the chord. Take a look at the two chord diagrams below—they are similar but different. These are the two basic shapes we will be using to play rhythm backup. There are many ways to identify these chord shapes, but to simplify things let's name them Shape 1 and Shape 2.

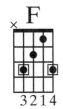

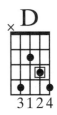

These are both major chords and the root note or name of the chord is indicated with a bold circle.

We've already used both of these shapes in "Salt Creek" (measures 3–4 and 11–12). To identify the chord in the first diagram above, we would call it "Shape 1 at the 3rd fret." In this case, we associate the chord shape with the 3rd fret because the lowest pitched note of the chord (the note being played on the 4th string) is on the 3rd fret. Similarly, the chord shown in the second diagram above would be called "Shape 2 at the 4th fret." These chord/fret designations are important because as we move the chords around the neck, their shapes remain the same but their letter names do not. For example, the chord in the first diagram is an F chord, or "Shape 1 at the 3rd fret." If we move it up a fret, it becomes an F♯ chord or "Shape 1 at the 4th fret." Move it up one more and it becomes a G chord, or "Shape 1 at the 5th fret." You get the idea.

To get started, make a G chord: Shape 1 at the 5th fret. It will look like this:

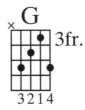

The basic rhythm pattern in the right hand is as follows: Thumb plays the 4th string on beat 1; then thumb, index, and middle pinch the 1st, 2nd, and 3rd strings together on beat 2; and then repeat, etc. It looks like this in tablature:

Example 41

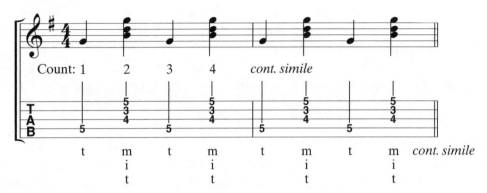

This pattern is very similar to the pinch roll you learned at the beginning of the book. The difference is that when you play this pattern, you need to make the pinches on beats 2 and 4 short, instead of letting them ring out. You can achieve this by lifting your left hand slightly but not removing it from the strings completely, just enough to cut off the ringing of the chord. The idea is to create a steady, pulsating rhythm that clearly defines the beat. This is called vamping.

Example 42

Now you're ready to move this chord shape around the neck a little bit. In this example, start with Shape 1 at the 5th fret (G chord) for two measures, then move to the 10th fret (C chord) for two measures, and then up to the 12th fret (D chord) for two measures. Try to keep the right-hand pattern steady as you switch from one chord position to another.

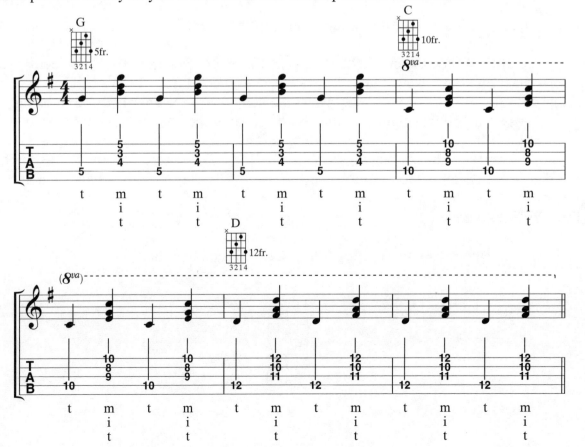

Example 43

Try this same chord progression again, but use Shape 2. Start with Shape 2 at the 9th fret (G chord) and then move to the 14th fret (C chord) and on to the 16th fret (D chord).

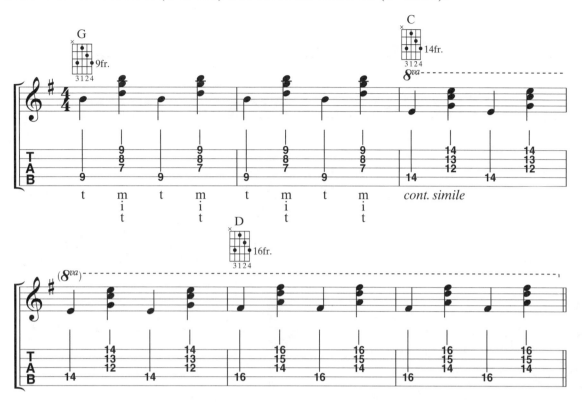

Example 44

Now we'll mix and match the same progression (G to C to D) but using one measure of Shape 1 and one measure of Shape 2 for each chord change.

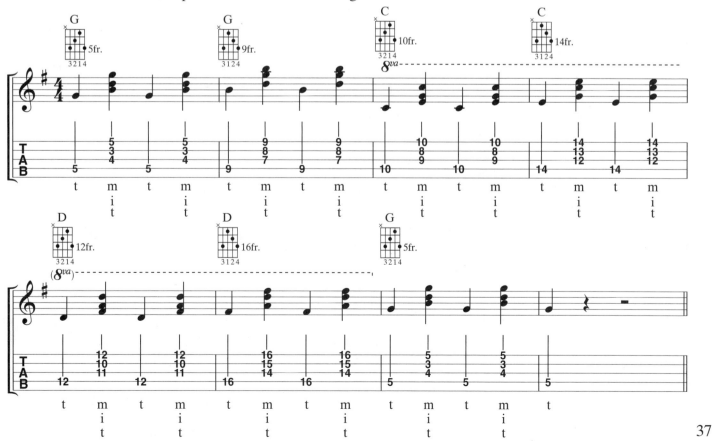

As you can tell, there are many different combinations and variations possible here. The idea is for you to become so familiar with a song's chord progression that you can switch between shapes and positions at will. As you learn more and more chords, your options will keep growing. For now, you will use the above shapes and patterns to play backup along with the tunes you've already learned:

Example 45: "Boil the Cabbage Down" – Vamp

Example 46: "Cripple Creek" – Vamp

CRIPPLE CREEK

TRADITIONAL

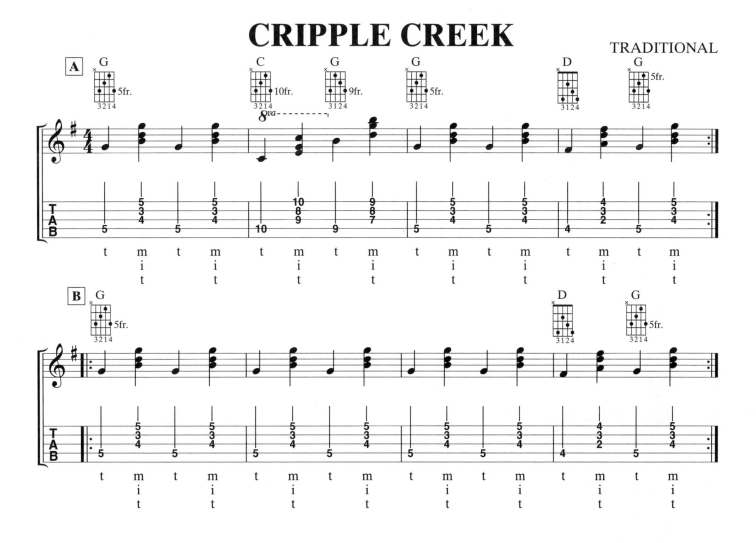

Example 47: "Cumberland Gap" – Vamp

CUMBERLAND GAP

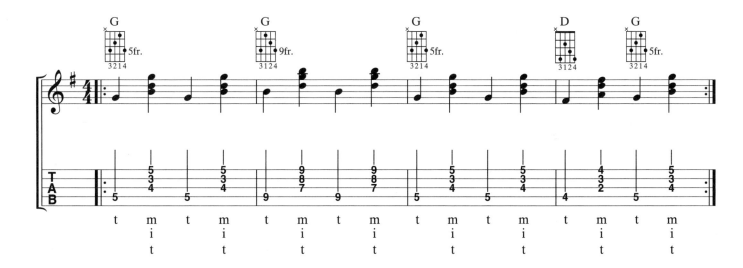

OLD JOE CLARK

TRADITIONAL

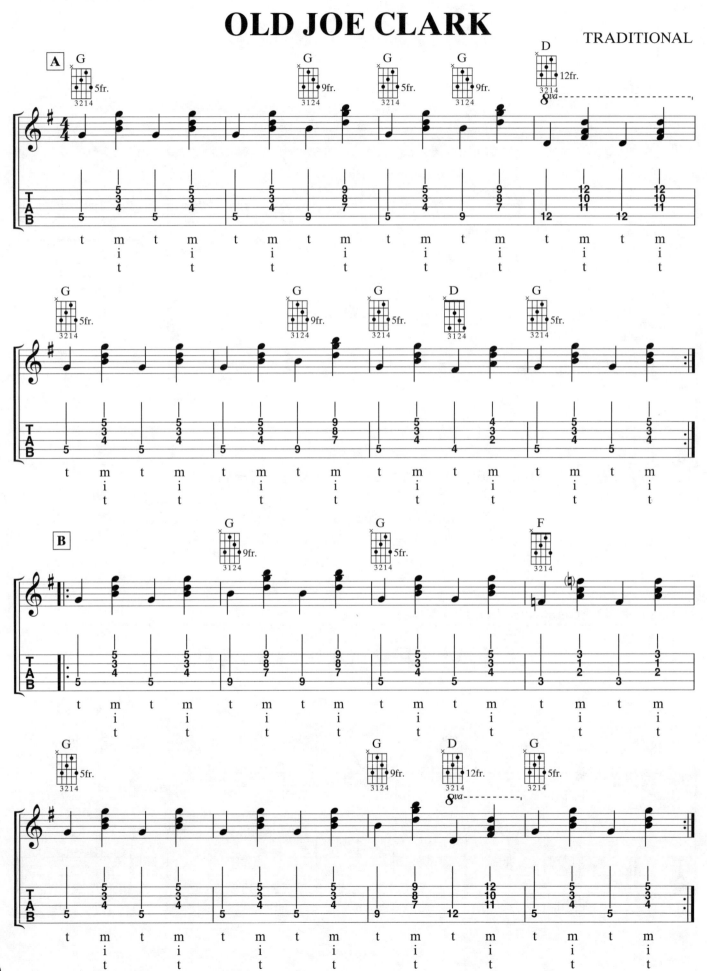

SALT CREEK

TRADITIONAL

Example 50: "John Hardy" – Vamp

JOHN HARDY

TRADITIONAL

UNIT 6: PLAYING UP THE NECK

Now that you've had some experience moving these chord shapes up and down the neck, try picking a few tunes that include some up-the-neck melody sections. Pay close attention to the left-hand fingering diagrams. This next tune is a favorite among guitar pickers. Here's "Wildwood Flower."

In measure 6 (second ending) play the notes on the 1st string (5th and 7th frets) with the ring finger of your left hand. This will set you up nicely to get the new left-hand position in measure 7 (letter B).

Example 51: "Wildwood Flower"

Next is an old-time fiddle tune that has become a bluegrass classic—"Sally Goodin." This arrangement uses several new left-hand positions. Section A is based on this position.

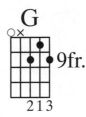

To play measures 1–3 of Section A, leave your fingers down in the position shown above, but reach up with your pinky finger to get the notes at the 10th and 11th frets of the 2nd string like this:

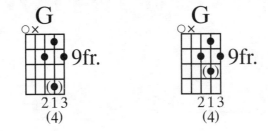

To start measure 4 of Section A, move your index finger from the 2nd string to the 3rd string like this:

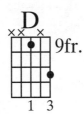

This may seem a bit confusing, but just pay close attention to the chord diagrams and you'll see the logic here. Notice that throughout Section A, your left-hand ring finger **never** leaves the 9th fret on the 1st string. Section B starts with these two positions:

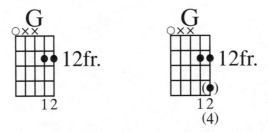

Keep your left-hand index and middle fingers down in measures 5–6 (first two measures of Section B) and reach up to get the note on the 14th fret with your left-hand pinky finger. Measures 7 and 8 are exactly like the last two measures of Section A. Take it slowly at first and don't forget about the right-hand timing. Count!

Example 52: "Sally Goodin"

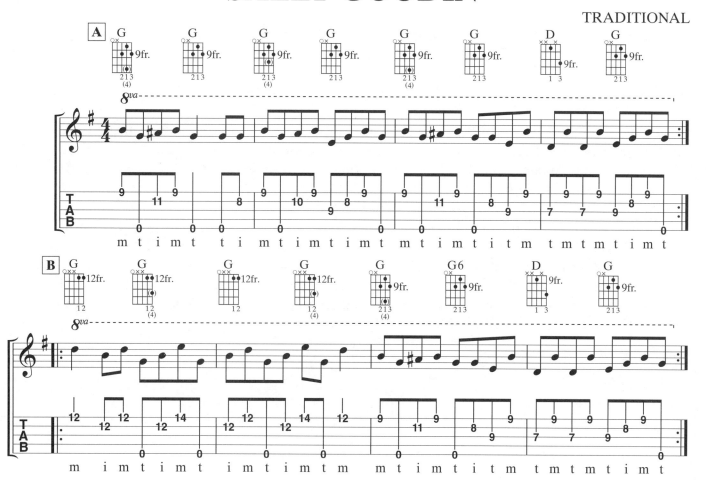

Example 53: "Cumberland Gap" (Section B)

Now we'll revisit one of the tunes you've already learned: "Cumberland Gap." You already know how to play Section A, but Section B is up the neck and uses the same positions as "Sally Goodin."

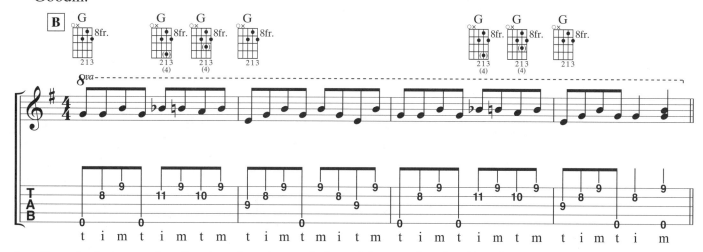

To play the whole tune, play Section A twice and then this new Section B twice: AABB.
The backup for Section B is the same as the backup for Section A.

Example 54: "John Henry"

We've had a song about an outlaw, now here's one about a railroad man, "John Henry." This old folk ballad has many verses and is a bluegrass standard. All the tunes you've learned up to now have been in the key of G, but this one is in the key of D. In order to play this tune, you need to raise the pitch of the 5th string from G to A. The best way to do this is with a 5th-string capo or spikes (see section "Using a Capo"), but if you don't have either you can just tune the string up to an A note (match the open 5th string to the 1st string at the 7th fret). The other four strings should remain in standard G tuning.

- In measures 3, 11, 13, and 17 there is a lick that involves a pull-off on the 2nd string. To do this, place your left-hand index finger on the 5th fret and your middle finger on the 6th fret at the same time. When you pull off the middle finger, your index will already be in place. This is similar to other pull-offs you've done on the 3rd string.

- Also, in measure 18 there is a note with this symbol (~) over the top (3rd fret of the 4th string). This is the symbol for a bend or choke. To do this just fret the note normally with the middle finger of your left hand and then just pull it a little bit toward the palm of your hand before you release it. This creates an interesting bluesy sound. Remember, practice this move slowly at first and work it into your right-hand roll. Don't sacrifice the timing of the roll for the choke. This tune is usually played quite fast; speed will come, but only after you've practiced slowly and cleanly first.

JOHN HENRY

⑤ = A

TRADITIONAL

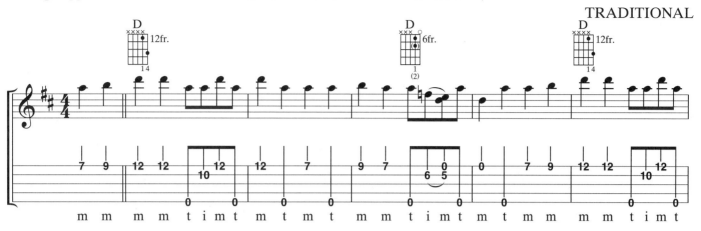

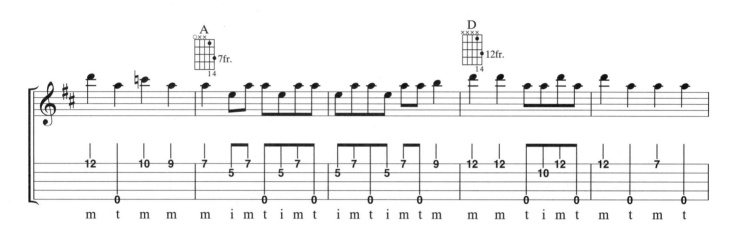

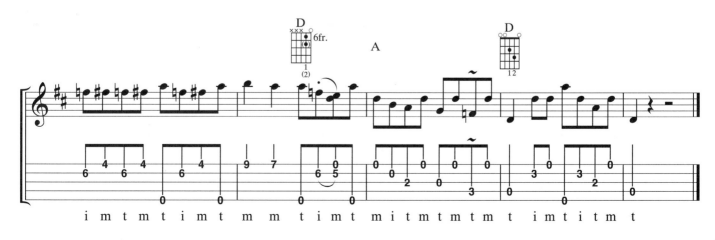

47

"Lonesome Road Blues" is another bluegrass banjo standard. We're back in standard G tuning for this one, so bring your 5th string back down to a G note. This tune starts with a slide on the 2nd string. Use your left-hand index finger to fret these first notes, and be sure to play the slide with the correct timing. Count! Pay attention to the chord diagrams for help with left-hand fingering. Once again, you are choking some notes in measures 3 and 11, so watch for the symbol (~) and keep your timing steady. You'll recognize the "Sally Goodin" position as well as some other positions you've already seen.

Example 55: "Lonesome Road Blues"

C Tuning

Now here's a tune in C tuning: Drop the 4th string from a D note down to a C note (one whole step down). Everything else stays the same. Earl Scruggs used this tuning quite a bit when playing in the key of C. This one is a favorite among fiddlers and a great tune to jam with because everyone knows it.

Example 56: "Soldier's Joy"

Play the slides in measures 1, 3, and 5 with your left-hand middle finger and be sure to make them last for their full duration. Watch your right-hand rolls closely, and count.

SOLDIER'S JOY

TRADITIONAL

Example 57: "Soldier's Joy" (backup)

For the backup on this tune, you're going to try a different approach. Instead of playing straight rhythm, play some rolls through the chord changes. This is a simple technique that sounds great behind the fiddle, especially if there are other instruments in the band already playing rhythm.

SOLDIER'S JOY

TRADITIONAL

Waltz (3/4) Time

Everything you've learned so far has been in 4/4 or common time: four beats to a measure. Many tunes in the bluegrass repertoire are in 3/4 or waltz time, where there are only three beats per measure. This next one is an old gospel tune called "Amazing Grace." This tune is also in the key of C, but this time you're in standard G tuning, so make sure your 4th string is back up to a D note. Since you're in a new time signature (3/4), pay special attention to your counting. Even though you're still using some of the same right-hand rolls you've always used, they somehow "feel" different when playing in 3/4 time:

Example 58: "Amazing Grace"

In the second-to-last measure (15), hold a complete C chord in your left hand and just reach over with your left-hand pinky finger to get the 3rd fret note on the 4th string. That way you'll already be in position for the last C chord.

51

Example 59: "Amazing Grace" (backup)

Playing rhythm backup in ¾ time is similar to 4/4 except that you play the single bass note on the 4th string and then play two pinches on beats 2 and 3: single note, pinch, pinch, single note, pinch, pinch, etc. Notice that in measure 14 you play a C chord on beats 1 and 2 and then change quickly to a 9th-fret G chord for just one beat and then back to the C chord. Keep the beat nice and even. Count!

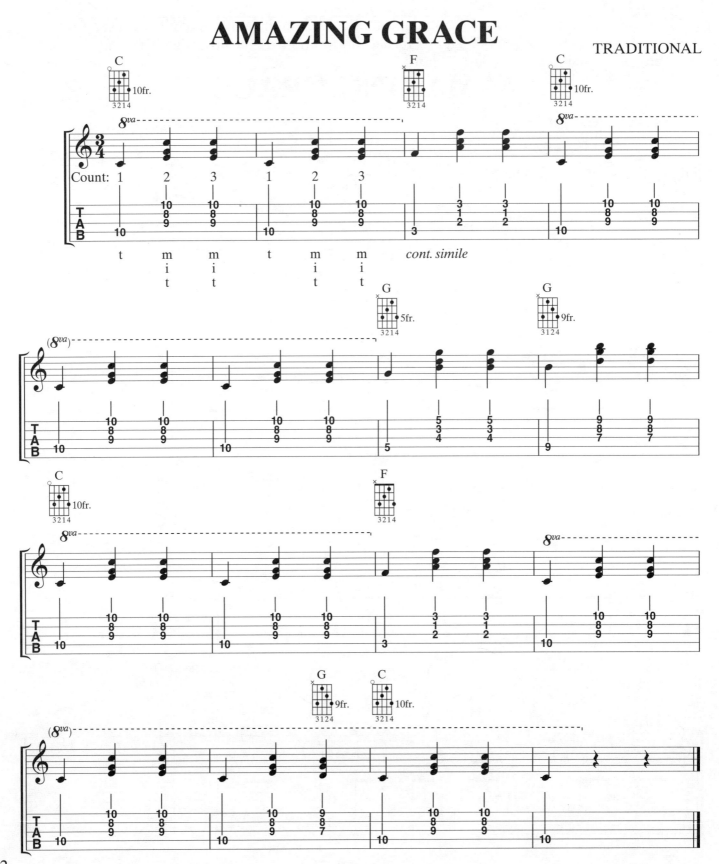

52

Endings

Here are a couple of Scruggs-style endings you can use for any instrumental tune in the key of G.
Usually if you are jamming and you take the last solo on a song, you will be expected to play the ending.
These are all four measures long and are based on a double shave-and-a-haircut ending.

Example 60

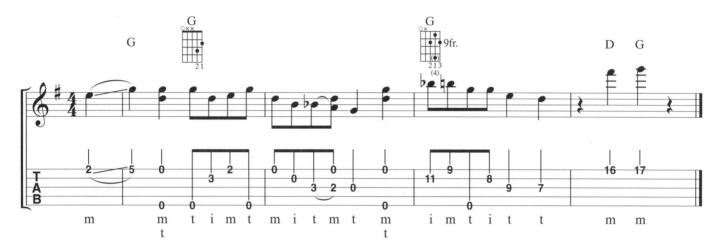

Example 61

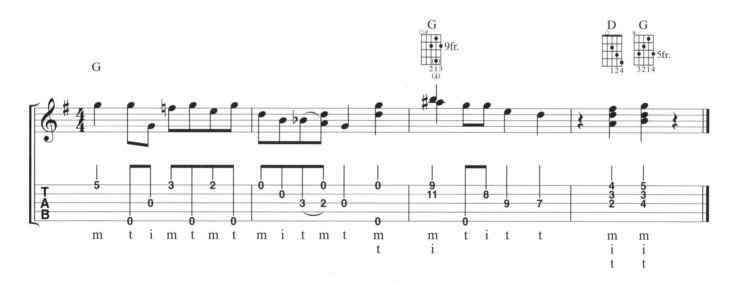

UNIT 7: MELODIC-STYLE BANJO

Now that you've studied the Scruggs style for a while, let's move on to a different kind of three-fingered picking commonly called melodic style. What is the difference between these styles? If you remember the initial discussion of the Scruggs style, you'll remember that the melody is played as a part of a roll. The melody notes are there, but they're surrounded by the other notes of the roll, which sort of fill in the spaces. In the melodic style, *every* note you play is a melody note. In general, there are no filler notes. Think of how a fiddle might play a tune—every note is a melody note. In fact, some people call this way of playing fiddle-tune style. No matter what you call it, it is definitely different from the Scruggs style and requires the use of some different left-hand positions and right-hand rolls. Let's look at the same tune played in both styles. Here is the first part of "Old Joe Clark" in the Scruggs style:

Example 62A: "Old Joe Clark" (Scruggs style)

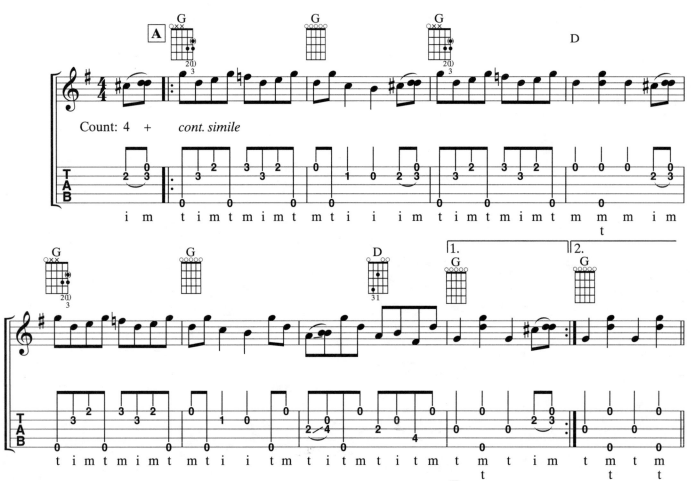

OLD JOE CLARK

TRADITIONAL

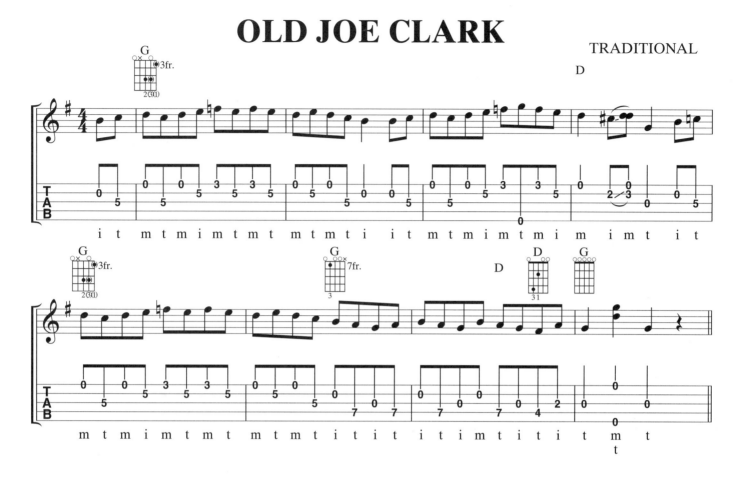

As you can hear, the melody is there in both versions, even though they are very different. Both styles have their uses; some songs sound great played in the Scruggs style and not so good in the melodic style. Other songs (especially fiddle tunes) can be rather difficult to play in the Scruggs style but lay out very nicely using the melodic style. "Old Joe Clark" happens to be great in either style.

When you're working your way through these tunes, pay close attention to the chord diagrams as well as the right-hand fingerings. Everything discussed with regard to learning the Scruggs style still applies here. If you're having difficulty, slow down and work on each hand separately. Count!

Let's start with a melodic version of "Cripple Creek."

Example 63: "Cripple Creek" (Melodic style)

CRIPPLE CREEK

TRADITIONAL

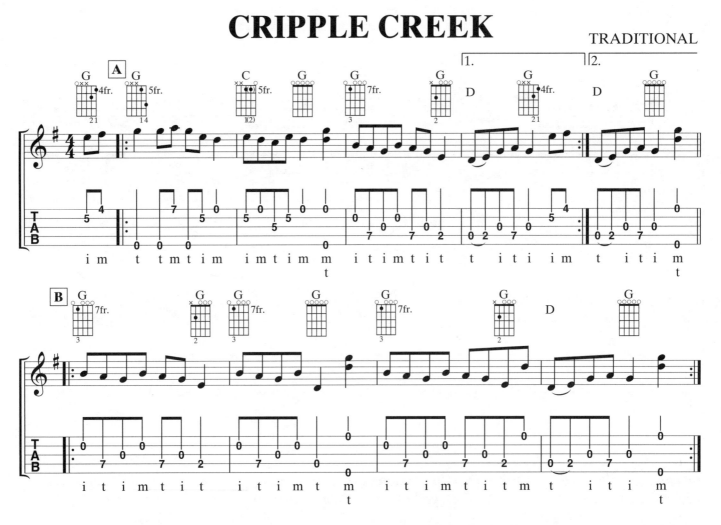

The new left-hand positions here are easy, but the right-hand roll is tricky in places. In measures 3, 6, 7, and 8 you need to play the 2nd string with your right-hand middle finger. This will take some getting used to because up to now you've used only the middle finger on the 1st string. To practice this technique you can play some forward or backward rolls on the inside strings like this:

CD
54A
Example 64A

CD
54B
Example 64B

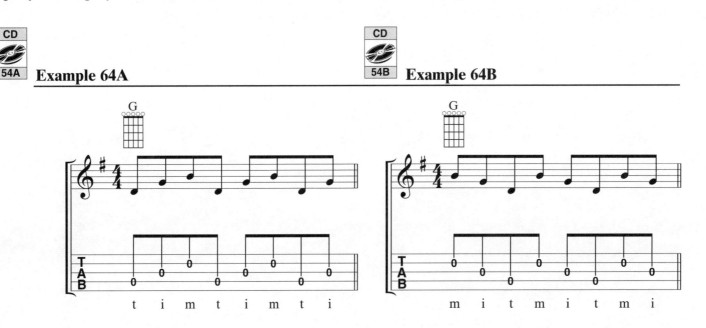

Example 65: "Whiskey Before Breakfast"

Here's a great Irish-sounding tune, "Whiskey Before Breakfast." Section B has a neat descending melody line in the last four measures. This is another very popular jamming tune and is usually played at a medium tempo.

Example 66: "Blackberry Blossom"

This is probably the all-time favorite melodic jam tune for banjo players. Section A is in the key of G and Section B is in E minor. This tune has a great melody and a very active chord progression (especially in Section A).

BLACKBERRY BLOSSOM

TRADITIONAL

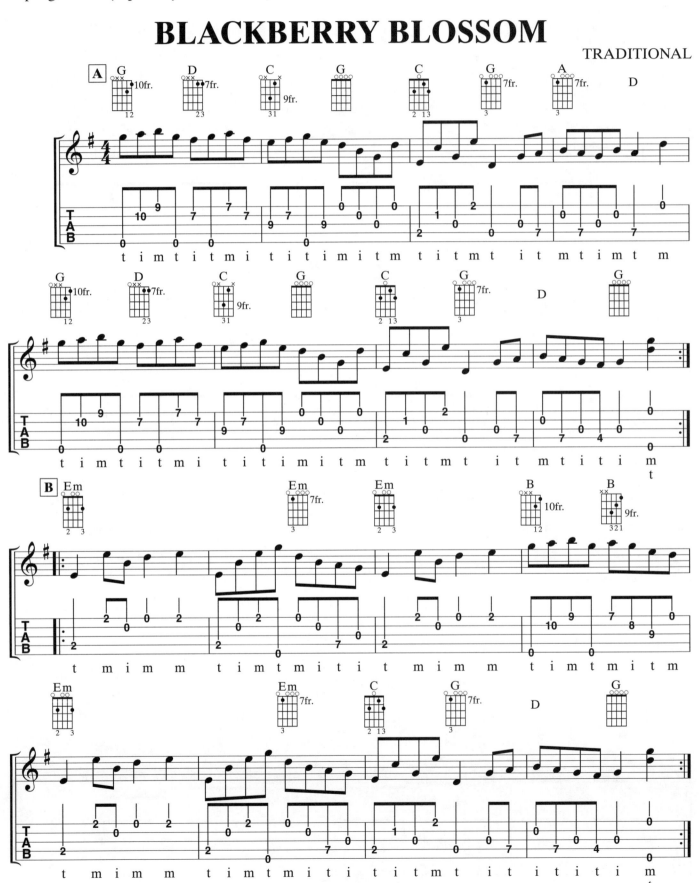

Example 67: "Blackberry Blossom" (backup)

BLACKBERRY BLOSSOM

TRADITIONAL

59

Example 68: "Blackberry Blossom" (backup with rolls)

Another way to back up this tune (especially behind the fiddle) is to use exactly the same chord positions as in Example 79, but roll through them instead of playing straight rhythm. In fact, now that you have the hang of playing rhythm, you should try rolling through all of the backup parts to all of the songs you've learned. You'll be surprised at some of the sounds you can come up with!

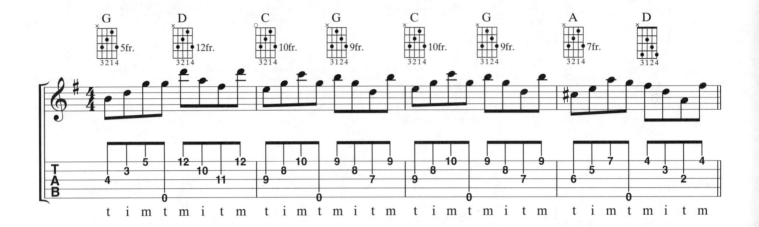

UNIT 8: COMBINING SCRUGGS AND MELODIC STYLES

By now you have a pretty good idea of the differences between the Scruggs and melodic styles of picking. Now try a few tunes where you combine the two styles. The idea here is to think of the two styles as tools you can use to articulate your musical ideas. You studied them independently in order to learn the basics of both, but the real fun happens when you can use them both together to make the music happen. This tune is the old Civil War song "Dixie."

Example 69: "Dixie"

DIXIE

TRADITIONAL

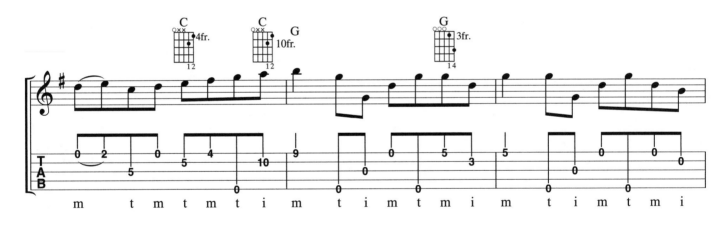

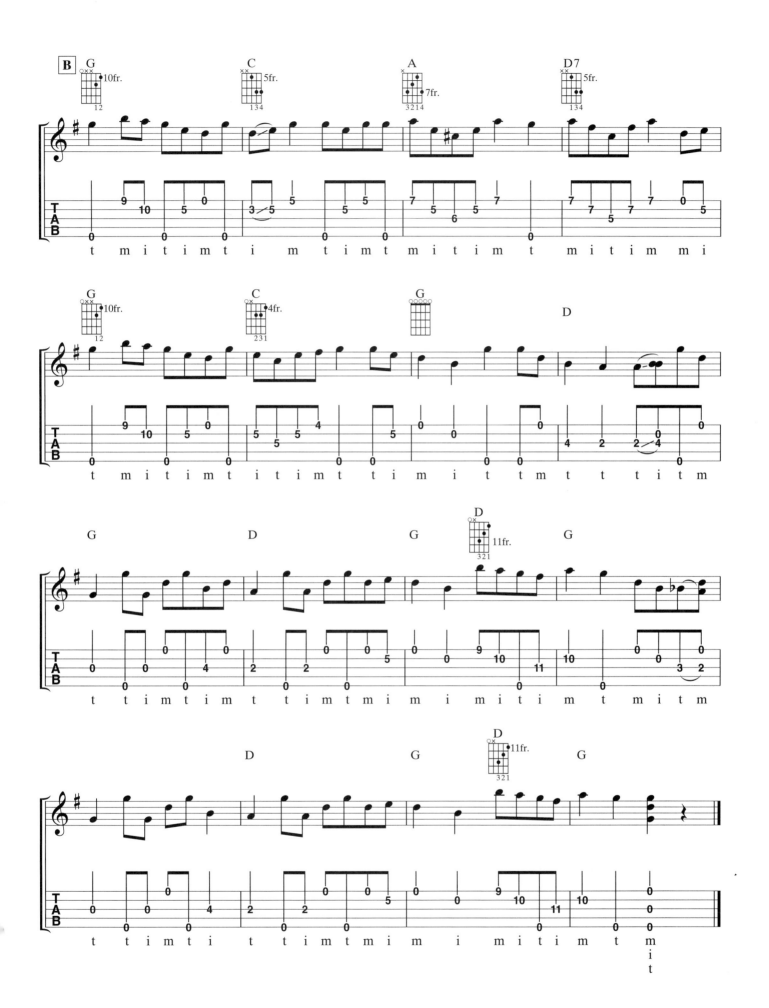

Example 70: "Black Mountain Rag"

"Black Mountain Rag" is an old fiddle tune that has become a jamming favorite. Flatpicking guitarists especially seem to like this one, and it makes a great banjo tune as well. There are three sections to this tune, with Sections A and B both having the same chord progression. For this reason, it can be tricky to play backup along with this one; only Section C, the third section, goes to the C chord. Watch the pickup note at the beginning; it occurs on the "and" of beat 4. In fact, all of the slides in Section A happen on the "and" of beat 4. Take it slowly, and count! There are some new left-hand shapes in this version, so watch those chord diagrams

BLACK MOUNTAIN RAG

TRADITIONAL

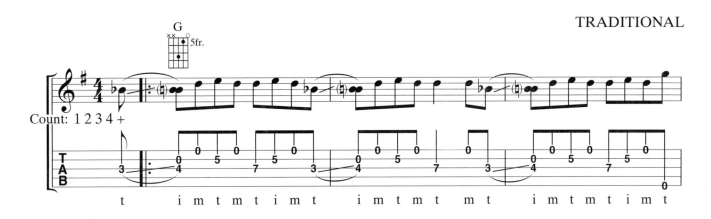

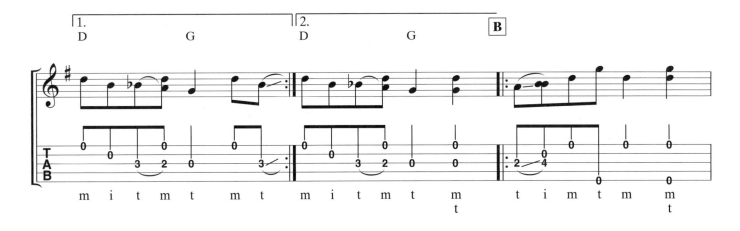

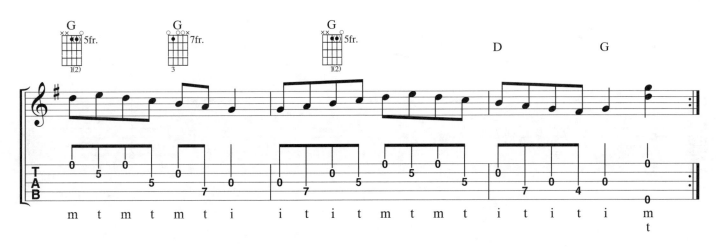

UNIT 9: USING A CAPO

Sometimes when you're playing with other people, you will find that you may know the same tunes but in different keys. For example, you learned "Boil the Cabbage Down" in G because it plays well on the banjo in that key. Most fiddlers play it in A, however. The same is true of many of the tunes in this book. In order to get around this problem, you can use a capo—a device that clamps on the neck of the banjo and raises the pitch of the strings. The capo is really like a moveable nut; it allows you to play the same fingerings but they sound in a higher key. To play "Boil the Cabbage Down" with a fiddler, you would just attach the capo at the 2nd fret and play your usual version of the tune using the same fingerings, but it will sound in the key of A rather than G.

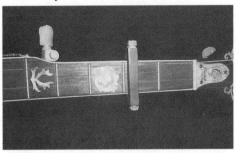

This works fine for the lower four strings, but the 5th string presents a problem. In order to raise the pitch of the 5th string, you can use a sliding 5th-string capo:

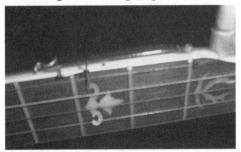

Or you can use a series of small hooks (actually miniature model railroad spikes) in the neck underneath the 5th string. For example, when you capo at the 2nd fret, you just slip the 5th string under the spike at the 7th fret, thus raising it two frets to match the other strings. Most new banjos made today use this system and come from the maker with these spikes already installed:

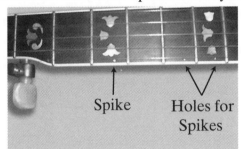

You will need to use a capo to play along with the full band versions of some of the tunes on the accompanying CD. In the list that follows you will find instructions on where to place the capo for each tune, if needed.

CD SONG LIST FOR FULL BAND ARRANGEMENTS

The following is a list of the band tunes on the CD. After each title, you will find the actual key in which the tune is being played and information on placement of your capo, if needed. Also included is the order of solos for the tune. The arrangements will give you the feel of playing in a jam session or band context. Whichever instrument takes the last solo will end the tune. The banjo follows the tablature in the book. Remember, if you want to remove the banjo from the mix and hear just the other instruments in the band, pan the music hard left. To hear only the banjo, pan hard right.

Boil the Cabbage Down: Key of A, banjo capo at 2nd fret, 5th string at 7th fret
Solos: fiddle, banjo, mandolin, guitar, fiddle.

Cripple Creek: Key of A, banjo capo at 2nd fret, 5th string at 7th fret
Solos: banjo, fiddle, mandolin, guitar, banjo.

Old Joe Clark: Key of A, banjo capo at 2nd fret, 5th string at 7th fret
Solos: fiddle, banjo, mandolin, guitar, fiddle.

Salt Creek: Key of A, banjo capo at 2nd fret, 5th string at 7th fret
Solos: banjo, fiddle, mandolin, guitar, banjo.

John Henry: Key of D, banjo capo 5th string only at 7th fret
Solos: guitar, banjo, mandolin, fiddle, guitar.

John Hardy: Key of G
Solos: guitar, banjo, mandolin, fiddle, guitar.

Wildwood Flower: Key of C, capo banjo at 5th fret, 5th string at 10th fret
Solos: guitar, banjo, mandolin, fiddle, guitar.

Sally Goodin: Key of A, banjo capo 2nd fret, 5th string at 7th fret
Solos: fiddle, banjo, mandolin, guitar, fiddle.

Cumberland Gap: Key of A, banjo capo 2nd fret, 5th string at 7th fret
Solos: banjo, fiddle, mandolin, guitar, banjo.

Lonesome Road Blues: Key of G
Solos: banjo, fiddle, mandolin, guitar, banjo.

Amazing Grace: Key of D, banjo capo 2nd fret, 5th string at 7th fret
Solos: mandolin, fiddle, banjo, guitar, mandolin.

Soldier's Joy: Key of D, banjo in C tuning, capo at 2nd fret, 5th string at 7th fret
Solos: fiddle, banjo, mandolin, guitar, fiddle.

Whiskey Before Breakfast: Key of D, banjo capo at 2nd fret, 5th string at 7th fret
Solos: mandolin, guitar, fiddle, banjo, mandolin.

Blackberry Blossom: Key of G
Solos: guitar, fiddle, mandolin, banjo, guitar.

Dixie: Key of G
Solos: banjo, mandolin, guitar, fiddle, banjo.

Black Mountain Rag: Key of A, banjo capo 2nd fret, 5th string at 7th fret
Solos: guitar, fiddle, mandolin, banjo, guitar.

APPENDIX 1

Reading Music Notation

Music is written on a **staff.** The staff consists of five lines and four spaces between the lines:

The names of the notes are the same as the first seven letters of the alphabet: A B C D E F G.

The notes are written in alphabetical order. The first (lowest) line is E:

Notes can extend above and below the staff. When they do, **ledger lines** are added. Here is the approximate range of the banjo from the lowest note, open 4th string D to a C on the 1st string at the 22nd fret.

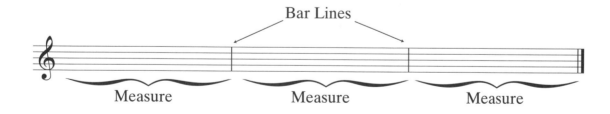

The staff is divided into **measures** by **bar lines.** A heavy double bar line marks the end of the music.

Rhythm Notation and Time Signatures

At the beginning of every song is a time signature. $\frac{4}{4}$ is the most common time signature.

4 FOUR COUNTS TO A MEASURE
4 A QUARTER NOTE RECEIVES ONE COUNT

The top number tells you how many counts per measure.
The bottom number tells you which kind of note receives one count.

The time value of a note is determined by three things:

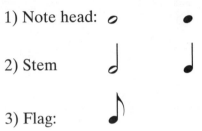

1) Note head: ○ ●

2) Stem

3) Flag:

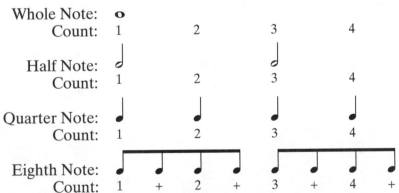

Whole Note:	○			
Count:	1	2	3	4
Half Note:				
Count:	1	2	3	4
Quarter Note:				
Count:	1	2	3	4
Eighth Note:				
Count:	1 +	2 +	3 +	4 +

Count out loud and clap the rhythm to this excerpt from "Jingle Bells."

Four Counts Per Measure

Jin -	gle	bells!		Jin -	gle	bells!		Jin -	gle	all	the	way!			
1	2	3	4	1	2	3	4	1	2	3	4	1	2	3	4

A Quarter Note Receives One Count

APPENDIX 3

Reading Tablature and Fingerboard Diagrams

Tablature illustrates the location of notes on the neck of the banjo. This illustration compares the five strings of a banjo with the five lines of tablature.

 Notes are indicated by placing fret numbers on the strings. An "O" represents an open string.

This tablature indicates to play the open, 2nd, and 3rd frets on the first string.

Tablature is usually used in conjunction with standard music notation. The rhythms and note names are indicated by the standard notation, and the location of those notes on the banjo neck is indicated by the tablature.

1st string
2nd string
3rd string
4th string
5th string

Chords are often indicated in **chord block diagrams.** The vertical lines represent the strings, and the horizontal lines represent the frets.

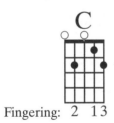

Fingering: 2 13

About the Author

Dennis Caplinger is a multitalented musician who has toured and recorded with many different artists, including Bluegrass Etc., Vince Gill, Chris Hillman and Herb Pedersen, Byron Berline, Dan Crary, Richard Greene, Chris Thile, Sean Watkins, John Reischman, Ray Park, Jann Browne, Kevin Welch, Kelly Willis, Ray Price, Rita Coolidge, and the Academy of Country Music Awards Show Band. His busy touring schedule as banjoist/fiddler with Bluegrass Etc. has taken him all over the world and yielded three critically acclaimed albums to date; their latest, *Home Is Where the Heart Is,* was voted one of the top ten bluegrass recordings of 1999 by the *Chicago Tribune.* A highly sought-after player/producer on the West Coast studio scene, he has worked on countless jingles, commercials, cartoons, and movies and has his own production company based in Vista, California. He is under contract with Network Productions of San Diego, California, recording TV and radio commercials as well as writing and recording for their extensive music library, one of the largest in the world. Dennis is actively producing and playing on projects for CMH records' popular *Pickin' On* series. Featured records he has been a part of include tributes to Eric Clapton, Santana, Creed, the Rolling Stones, Led Zeppelin, Bonnie Raitt, Jim Morrison, Queen, Neil Diamond, the Dave Matthews Band, R.E.M., ZZ Top, Lynyrd Skynyrd, the Black Crowes, Phish, Dolly Parton, Brooks and Dunn, Lonestar, Lee Ann Womack, Jo Dee Messina, and Tim McGraw. His movie soundtrack credits include *Back to the Future III, El Diablo, Rio Diablo,* and Steven King's *Apt Pupil,* among others. Dennis's playing is featured on the soundtrack of "The Simpsons" and Warner Bros. cartoons "Pinky and the Brain" and "Histeria" as well as numerous programs on PBS, A&E, TNN, and the History Channel. Recent commercials include those for New York Life, Supercuts, Subway, Discover Card featuring John Lithgow, and Cingular Wireless, in which Dennis appeared along with Bluegrass Etc. Dennis has contributed to *Banjo Newsletter* and can be seen in the October 1999 issue of *Bluegrass Now* magazine, which contains a feature article on him.